Excel Macros

Step by Step Tutorial on How to Make and Record Excel Macros

Edward Fish

Copyright@2019

TABLE OF CONTENT

CHAPTER 1

INTRODUCTION

As humans, we derive pleasure in doing this, there are particular things that we do on a daily basis every working day, it would be amazing if there was a magical way of pressing a single button and all of our daily job would be done at once, in conclusion , a macro in the magical single button

Excel is filled with wonderful ways to save time such as keyboard shortcuts, the fill handle, templates and so on

But there is no better time saving tool than a macro!

In conclusion, a macro is a series of instructions that excel executes when you tell it to

And then it opens up a large number of possibilities

In this guide, you will be shown how to create macros on your own and how to run it

CHAPTER 2

WHAT IS A MACROS

A macros is a piece of programming code that runs in excel environment which helps to automate routine tasks, that is in a layman language, a macro is recording of your routine steps in Excel that you can replay making use of a single button

After you have created a macro, Excel will execute those instructions, step by step on any data that is provided

Example, we can have macro that tells Excel to take a number, add

3, multiplied by seven and return the modulus

Now, whenever we tell Excel to run that macro, we don't have to manually do each step, Excel will do them all

It may look like something very easy at first, but macros can help you save a big amount of time, if you do the same series of steps on regular basics

It can be used for formatting raw data, filtering and sorting information, or applying the same series of operations and functions to your sheets

And they are wonderful for sharing, this is because macros can be stored in Excel spreadsheets, you do not have to worry about sending extra files to your colleagues, you can simply write a macro, send the spreadsheet over and allow them work with it

If you work with spreadsheets on normal basics, there is a wonderful chance that you could save a lot of time by working with macros

CHAPTER 3

IMPORTANCE OF MACROS IN EXCEL

Assuming you work as a cashier for a water utility company, some customers pay through the bank and at the end of the day, you are asked to download the data from the bank and then format it in a format that meets your business requirement

You can choose to import the data into excel and then format, the following day, you will be asked to perform the same thing, after some time, it becomes tedious and boring

Macros helps to solve such problems by helping to automate such routine tasks, you can use macro to record the steps of

Helping to import data

Helping to format it to meet your business report requirement

CHAPTER 4

WHAT IS VBA

VBA is an acronym for Visual Basic for Applications; it is a programming language that Excel uses to record your steps as you perform routine tasks

You do not need to be a programmer or a very technical individual to enjoy the full benefits of macros in excel

Excel has features that automatically generate the code for you

MACRO BASICS

Macro is one of the developer features, by default, the tab for developers is not shown in excel, you will need to display it using a customized report

Macros can be used to prevent your system by attackers, by default, they are disabled in excel, if you have to run macros, you will need to enable running macros and ensure you use macros that is from a reliable source

If you want to save macros, then you will have to save your workbook in a macro enabled format *.xlsm

The macro name should not contain any spaces

Ensure you always fill in the description of the macro when you create one; this will enabled you and others to understand what the macro is doing

CHAPTER 5

STEP BY STEP EXAMPE OF RECORDING MACROS IN EXCEL

We will work with the example described in the importance of macros excel, we will work with the CSV file shown below

```
serial no,date,account no,amount
1,01-02-2015,001,500
2,01-02-2015,001,200
3,01-02-2015,001,350
4,01-02-2015,001,2500
5,01-02-2015,001,5000
```

We will create a macro enabled template that will import the above data and then format it to meet our business and reporting requirements

CHAPTER 6

ENABLE DEVELOPER OPTION

For you to execute VBA program, you have to have access to developer option in Excel, you have to Enable the developer option as shown below and then pin it into your main ribbon in Excel

The following is the procedure to do this

Step 1

Start by going to the main menu "File" and selection option "Options"

Step 2

Next select "Options" from the menu list as shown in the screenshot below

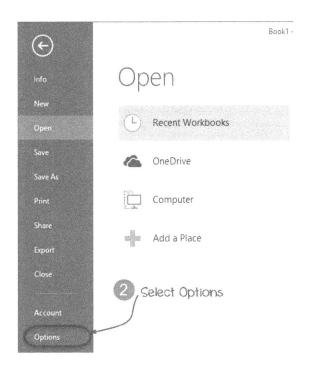

Step 3

Next another window will open and in that window do the following things

*Click on Customize Ribbon

*Next mark the checker box for Developer option

Next click on OK button

Step 4

it will display the DEVELOPER tab present in the ribbon

First, we will now see how we can create a command button on the

spreadsheet and execute the program

Paste the receipts.csv file that you download

1

Click on the DEVELOPER tab

2

Click on Record Macro as shown below

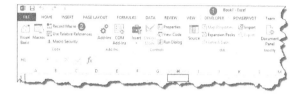

You will then see the following dialogue window

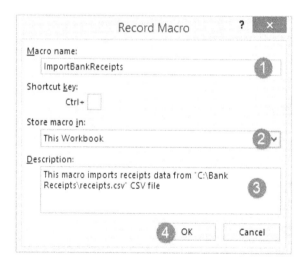

1

Next enter ImportBankReceipts as the macro name

2

Step 2 will be there by default

3

Next enter the description as shown in the above diagram

4

Click on "OK" tab

Next put the cursor in cell A1

Click on the DATA tab

Next click on from Text button on the Get External data ribbon bar

You will see the following
dialogue window

*Move to the local drive where
CSV file is stored

*Next select the CSV file

*Next click on Import button

You will see the following wizard

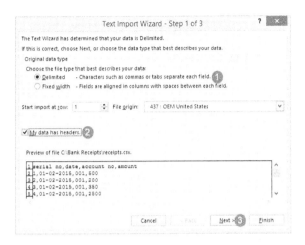

Click on the Next button after you follow the above steps

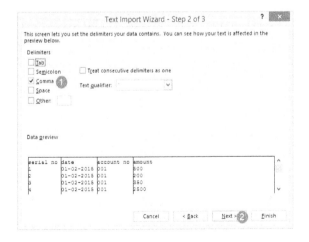

Next follow the above steps and click on next button

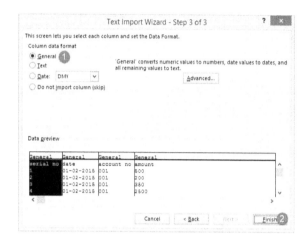

*Next Click on Finish button

*your workbook will look like this

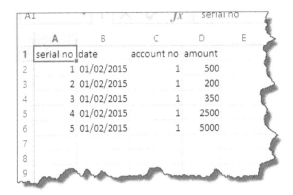

Next make the columns bold, and then add the grand total and then use the SUM function to get the total amount

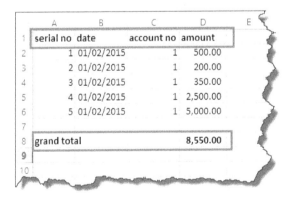

Now that we have concluded our routine work, we can click on stop recording macro button as shown in the image below

Before we save our workbook, we will have to delete the imported data, we can do this to create a template that we will be copying each time we have a new receipt and want to run the ImportBankReceipts macro

*Start by highlighting all the imported data

*Next right click on the
highlighted data

*Click on Delete

*Click on save as button

*Save the workbook in the macro
format used as highlighted below

Make a copy of the newly saved
template

Open it

Next click on DEVELOPER tab

Click on Macros button

You will get the following dialogue window

Select ImportBankReceipts

Next highlight the description of your macro

Next click on Run button

You will get the following data

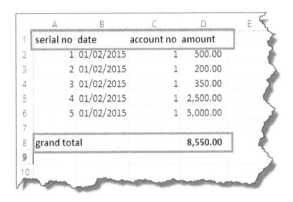

	A	B	C	D	E
1	serial no	date	account no	amount	
2	1	01/02/2015	1	500.00	
3	2	01/02/2015	1	200.00	
4	3	01/02/2015	1	350.00	
5	4	01/02/2015	1	2,500.00	
6	5	01/02/2015	1	5,000.00	
7					
8	grand total			8,550.00	
9					
10					

Congratulation, you have just created your first macro in excel

CONCLUSION

Macros help to simplify our work
and life by helping to automate
most of the routine works that we
do, Macro in excel are usually
powered by Visual Basic for
Application

THE END